CONSPIRACY FACT:
Human Experimentation in the United States

Kate Marcello

Disclaimer

Please keep in mind that the content of this publication is only as good as the information with which I have sourced it. This content is being presented as fact given the sources are facts.

Image credits: Wikipedia.org
Cover Images: ProWebWriter.com

Introduction
Mid-Nineteenth to Early Twentieth Century
    J. Marion Sims
    Dr. Robert Bartholow and Mary Rafferty
    Dr. Arthur Wentworth
    Dr. Leo Stanley
    Heinous Injectables
    Early Twentieth Century
    Tuskegee
World War II Era Through the Mid-Century
    Dr. Jonas Salk
    Dr. William C. Black
    Stateville Penitentiary
    Guatemala and Syphilis
    Dr. Joseph Stokes
    Willowbrook State School
    Sloan-Kettering Institute and Ohio State Prison
    Tampa Bay, Florida and the CIA
    Chester M. Southam
Government-Orchestrated Biological Warfare Tests
    Biological Attack Over San Francisco
    Operation Big Itch and Operation Big Buzz
    Project Shipboard Hazard and Defense (SHAD)
Human Radiation Testing
    Radioactive Iodine Tests
        The "Green Run"
        The Atomic Energy Commission
        Sonoma State Hospital
    Uranium Tests
        University of Rochester
        Dr. William Sweet
    Plutonium Tests and the Manhattan Project
        Albert Stevens
        Simeon Shaw

Elmer Allen
Testing Involving Other Radioactive Materials
    Vanderbilt University - Tennessee
    Walter E. Fernald State School - Massachusetts
    Medical College of Virginia
    Utah State Prison and the University of Utah
Irradiation Testing
    Department of Defense and Dr. Eugene L. Saenger
    Dr. Carl Heller and the Buchenwald Touch
Chemical Warfare Testing
    Mustard Gas
        Glenn Jenkins
        Nathan Schnurman
        Russell O'Berry
    Dermatological Testing
        Dr. Albert M. Kligman and Holmesburg Prison
Continued Experimentation
    If You Liked This Book
From the Author
Addendum
    Links From Book Text in Order of Appearance

If you enjoyed this book, please check out the next book in the series:

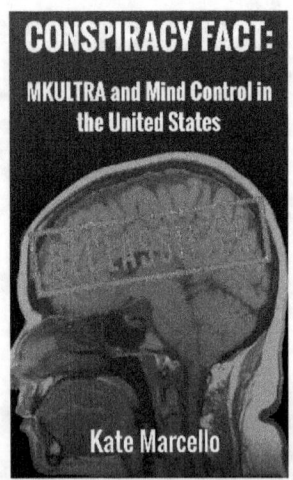

Mind Control in the United States?
Hard to believe? The series Conspiracy
Fact Declassified is back again to prove it
happened.

Through declassified documents and
various other sources, we further explore
human experimentation. This time we

zoom in specifically on mind control and the Top Secret government projects that examined this realm.

We name the names.

This compelling book is sourced throughout. You'll find out about how the U.S. ferried Nazi scientists into the country after World War II, and how that single operation became the catalyst for the creation of MULTIPLE experimental projects. You'll find out how those projects sourced more than 88 institutions nationwide to perform mind control experiments on unwitting citizens.

You will hear from survivors. Check it out on Amazon - http://amzn.to/1KzGGPL

Check out my blog: http://theydoconspire.blogspot.com/

Join the conversation on Facebook:

https://www.facebook.com/conspiracynontheories/

Introduction

The title of this book sounds like a bad dream or a conspiracy theory. I wish it were. The harsh reality is that the U.S. government has performed some heinous tests on citizens without their knowledge or consent. The extent of this testing sometimes resulted in negative effects for life and even death.

As if the horrors contained in these pages weren't bad enough, these tests and experiments were often performed on the poor, minorities, children, mentally ill, and powerless often under the guise of medical treatment.

Equally shocking is the fact that some of these atrocities occurred in many of our lifetimes, and the people and entities responsible have never been convicted of any crime. I assure you, much of what you're about to read does constitute criminal activity. It is also important to note that these experiments happened around the world although I am limiting this publication to those that occurred in the United States.

It is of utmost importance that Americans, and all world citizens be aware that these things happened. It is fact. It is NOT conspiracy theory. Not only did they happen, but efforts were made to conceal them from we the people. They were funded with your tax dollars. I ask you to consider...if your government would conduct these terrible things on the more vulnerable members of the population, why are conspiracy theorists constantly discredited and written off as nuts when they speak against government?

A government that could do these things to its citizens is most capable of anything.

NOTE: If you bought the print version of this book, all SOURCE links appear in the Addendum at the end for you research convenience.

Mid-Nineteenth to Early Twentieth Century

As technology steamed onward through the Industrial Age, science and medicine were also actively evolving. Early examples of human testing occurred just prior to and following the Civil War. At that time, modern medicine consisted of

hacking off a shrapnel-infested limb with a saw while the patient took a sip of whiskey and bit a stick in lieu of anesthesia. Enter the enslaved African, often considered the perfect test subject.

J. Marion Sims

J. Marion Sims conducted tests on enslaved African women through the 1840s. Sims was a pioneer in surgery and is referred to as the "father of modern gynecology" because of his innovations with a condition called vesicovaginal fistula. This condition accompanied childbirth and left women sufferers as social outcasts because of the symptoms which included leaking urine.

The problem with Sims was his use of a vulnerable population in order to achieve advances in medicine. Sims kept and owned up to 14 African women at one time with fistulas. The worst problem besides this by far was that Sims chose not to use anesthesia which was an available; albeit, new concept in modern medicine of the times. At least one of the women Sims kept was operated on 30 times. Many of the women became ill and died from complications for Sims' experiments. While many of his discoveries in this process were ground-breaking, the ethics with which they were conducted fall under severe moral scrutiny. This man valuated human beings, more specifically women, and when he ascertained them worth less, it became acceptable to him to inflict horrible pain and suffering unto death. There are many more like him to follow.

[Source]

Dr. Robert Bartholow and Mary Rafferty

In 1874, Dr. Bartholow met Mary Rafferty. Mary was a 30-year-old Irish woman who came to him for treatment for her cancer. She presented with a hole in her skull that was 2 inches in diameter caused by the cancer. Dr. Bartholow decided to apply a low electrical current to her exposed dura (brain) and noticed that it made various parts of Mary's body twitch and move. She complained of no pain, so Dr. Bartholow upped the current. Mary displayed distress at this and began to convulse violently. She was left in a comatose state for 3 days before she regained consciousness. The following day, she suffered a massive seizure and died.

Dr. Bartholow was criticized by the American Medical Association, but his career did not suffer as a result. He attained professional accolades through the late 1800s and died at his home in Philadelphia in 1904.

Perhaps Mary was seen as good as dead in any instance, but the fact that Dr. Bartholow was inspired to conduct this experiment based on experiments that were taking place at the time with animals, it's not as if he were lacking in subjects. It seems his decision was less than ethical from Mary's standpoint. [Source]

Dr. Arthur Wentworth

You wouldn't have wanted to be a patient at the Children's Hospital in Boston in 1896. It was then that Dr. Arthur Wentworth selected 29 children without parental consent on which to perform spinal taps. He sought to find out whether or not spinal taps were harmful. Can you imagine the outrage something like this would cause today or the lawsuits it would generate? It's ludicrous. Having had numerous spinal taps myself, I can tell you that they are quite unpleasant. They are also not a procedure that modern doctors seek to do without careful consideration because they are quite intrusive. There is a significant chance for infection and other complications.

[Source]

Dr. Leo Stanley

Dr. Leo Stanley was the chief surgeon at San Quentin State Penitentiary between 1913 and 1951. In a foreshadowing worthy of Nazi Germany, he conducted a wide array of experiments on hundreds of prisoners. Nearly all of his experiments centered around testicles and he believed he would revolutionize the rejuvenation of old men, control criminals, and prevent those he thought unworthy of reproduction.

His experiments involved such cringe-worthy things as implanting the testicles of executed prisoners into live ones, implanting animal testicles into prisoners, and he also participated in forced sterilizations of prisoners to carry out a burgeoning Eugenics agenda. Dr. Stanley ushered in the experimentation boom that came along with the second World War and saw America right into the mid-century while performing these horrors on a group that he obviously deemed as throwaways. [Source]

Heinous Injectables

The late 1800s saw an influx of conscious-less people who thought it'd be a great idea to test and experiment with sexually-transmitted diseases by injecting them into innocent people. It began in Hawaii with a Dr. George L. Fitch conducting a number of experiments among the native population who also suffered from Leprosy. He injected 6 girls under the age of 12 with syphilis in addition to other atrocities such as cutting a leprous piece of flesh from one person and transferring it to another. [Source]

A New York pediatrician, yes, a children's doctor, Dr. Henry Heiman decided it was cool to play around with gonorrhea cultures. He injected it into to 2 mentally-disabled boys; one was only 4 years old. In fact, in the late 1800s and early 1900s, more than 40 reports exist of people being intentionally infected with gonorrhea cultures. Some of these reports document where the gonorrheal organism was applied to the eyes of children. [Source]

I have trouble imagining a world where the cutting edge of any field would require the intentional infliction of serious disease and possible death on my fellow humans. In my simple understanding of innovation, I fail to see any advancement worth these acts of torture and terrorism. In today's world, we rant and rave over public beheadings, yet these experiments pepper our history.

Early Twentieth Century

The early twentieth century ushered in a solid 40 years of experimentation in some cases. In 1908 In Philadelphia, dozens of children at an orphanage were referred to as the "material used" in a study where they were injected with tuberculin. This resulted in painful lesions, inflammation of the eyes, and permanent blindness in many of the subjects. These were *children*. In addition to being unwanted, they were also deemed unworthy of their inalienable rights as humans in America. [Source]

Dr. Hideyo Noguchi was working on a skin test for syphilis comparable to the one used for tuberculosis in 1911 and

1912. He injected 146 patients with syphilis. Some of them were children. Some of the parents actually sued Dr. Noguchi and his experimentation became public scandal; however, the New York district attorney would not press charges, so nothing came of the case. [Source]

In fact, it would be late into the twentieth century before major laws prohibiting human experimentation would be passed. Can you believe that?

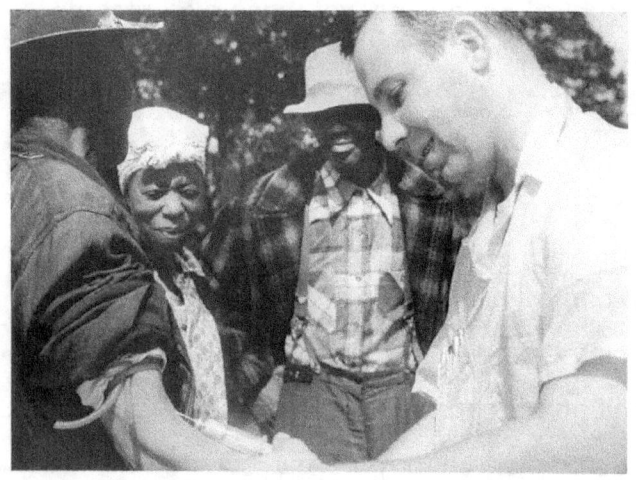

Tuskegee

Possibly one of the most shameful experiments in this publication due to the sheer longevity is the Tuskegee Syphilis Experiment. From 1932 to 1972, the United States Public Health Service in Tuskegee, Alabama conducted an experiment on 400 black males living in poverty who were infected with syphilis. The researchers "treated" the patients by essentially withholding treatment. In 1947 when penicillin was introduced, the patients were lied to about their condition and treatment so that the effects of the disease could be further observed. By 1972, only 74 of the men were still alive. 128 of the men had died of syphilis or related complications. 40 of their wives had contracted the disease which resulted in 19 children being born with congenital syphilis. The study was finally shut down at this point due to an outcry from the public...and rightly so!

[Source]

World War II Era Through the Mid-Century

During World War II, there was a technology race going on. Before the Space Race, there was the race to dominate rocket and medical science between the Allies and the Axis Powers. Major players were the United States, Germany, and Japan.

106 German rocket scientists. Fort Bliss, Texas 1945

At the end of the war, Operation Paperclip saw more than 1,500 Nazi scientists granted immunity and given asylum in the United States. The U.S. wanted Germany's scientists like Wernher Von Braun who would be instrumental in getting us to the moon first. The entire situation adds to a shameful past. [Source]

Dr. Jonas Salk

In 1941, a group of virologists that included Jonas Salk, famous for the polio vaccine, infected patients at local mental institutions with influenza while doing experiments for the University of Michigan. When attempting to publish the results of their experiments, they were cautioned by the editor of the Journal of Experimental Medicine, Francis Payton Rous, that they should publish elsewhere due to close scrutiny from groups against human experimentation. Rous advised that the "tests were wholly justified" in spite of his cautioning. [Source]

Dr. William C. Black

Rous flip-flopped his opinions when Dr. William C. Black inoculated a 12-month-old baby that was allegedly "offered as a volunteer" with the herpes virus. Rous called the experiment "an abuse of power" among other things. The study was then obviously rejected from the Journal of Experimental Medicine; however, it was published at a later date in the Journal of Pediatrics. [Source]

Stateville Penitentiary

The University of Chicago Medical School, in conjunction with the U.S. Army and the State Department conducted research at Stateville Penitentiary near Joliet, Illinois. The experiment consisted of a controlled study of the effects of malaria on prisoners there. This study went on for 29 years. [Source]

During this same time, Dr. Alf Alving was testing various malaria treatments on mental patients at Illinois State Hospital he had purposely infected with the disease. Needless to say, the study did not mention any means of gaining consent from the patients themselves. [Source]

Guatemala and Syphilis

Between 1946 and 1948, the U.S. Public Health Service worked with a number of health organizations and the Guatemalan government. They used prostitutes to infect Guatemalan prisoners, insane asylum patients, and soldiers with syphilis as well as other sexually-transmitted diseases. You know, because Tuskegee wasn't enough? The purpose was supposedly to test the effectiveness of penicillin on the diseases.

Later in the study, they went so far as to pour syphilis bacteria directly into men's penises, or into areas on patient's' arms or faces that had been abraded. In a few cases, they introduced the disease through lumbar puncture (spinal tap). So not only was a team of researchers conducting terrible experiments on humans, they were going about it without regard for the patient's' comfort or suffering. This team was lead by John Charles Cutter. Cutter would later go on to work on the Tuskegee Experiment as well. In 2010, the U.S. government apologized to Guatemala for the horrible testing. [Source]

Dr. Joseph Stokes

Dr. Stokes, as all of the other doctors in this publication, were required to take the Hippocratic oath promising to "first, do no harm". He intentionally injected 200 women prisoners with viral hepatitis in 1950. No doubt this was so he could complete some influential studies and papers detailing his research. [Source]

Willowbrook State School

Between the 1950s and 1972, research was conducted to find a vaccine for viral hepatitis. The methods of this research performed against mentally-disabled children are appalling. Children were deliberately infected with the disease. Even worse, from 1963 to 1966 parents were promised admission to Willowbrook for their children if they consented to "vaccines". These vaccines were viral infection of hepatitis via an extract fed to the children that was made from the feces of infected patients. [Source]

Sloan-Kettering Institute and Ohio State Prison

Knowing that injecting live cancer cells into healthy patients might cause cancer did not stop the researchers. In 1952, Chester M. Southam injected prisoners at Ohio State Prison. Southam was a Sloan-Kettering researcher, and the institute saw its share of unethical testing. 300 healthy women were injected with live cancer cells there without their knowledge.

Do you find it chilling at all that Sloan-Kettering is still active in cancer research as are many of the other facilities discussed in this book? [Source]

Tampa Bay, Florida and the CIA

There are conflicting sources and reports that state the CIA released whooping cough bacteria from boats moored in Tampa Bay in 1955. The result was an epidemic in the city that killed as many as 12 people. In my research, I came across sources debunking this claim; however, I also found some pretty solid sources corroborating the claims. Given where we are in this publication, it is easy to believe. [Source][Source]

Chester M. Southam

As if injecting prisoners and healthy women with live cancer cells weren't enough, Southam wasn't done after his tenure at the Sloan-Kettering Institute. A little over a decade later in 1963, he was at it again at the Jewish Chronic Disease Hospital in Brooklyn, New York. Southam injected 22 elderly patients at the hospital with live cancer cells in order to study how the healthy human body fought the invasion of cancerous cells. The hospital tried to cover up the study, but Southam was eventually placed on probation for a year by the New

York Medical Licensing Board. It had little effect on his career and he was elected as Vice President of the American Cancer Society two years later. Isn't it comforting to know that the leaders in cancer research and treatment learned what they know from such inhuman tests? [Source]

Government-Orchestrated Biological Warfare Tests

Biological Attack Over San Francisco

In 1950, the U.S. Navy sprayed the bacteria, serratia marcescens, which was thought to be harmless, over San Francisco. This caused pneumonia-like symptoms in a number of citizens and at least one death. Similar tests were conducted through at least 1969. [Source]

Operation Big Itch and Operation Big Buzz

Throughout the 1950s, the United States conducted a number of biological warfare tests which included entomological tests using insects to spread pathogens. Operation Big Itch involved uninfected fleas and was basically a test to determine if the insects could survive the munitions phase to go on to infect people. Operation Big Itch was conducted in Utah at the Dugway Proving Grounds in 1954. [Source]

The next year, the testing escalated. Citizens in parts of the state of Georgia became guinea pigs for a test where 300,000 mosquitoes infected with yellow fever were dropped from aircraft. Again, the purpose of the test was to see if the insects could survive the initial phase going on to bite and infect the population. [Source]

There were at least two other entomological warfare tests conducted as well: Operation Drop Kick and Operation May Day. Both tests used uninfected mosquitoes to test the spread of the insects throughout the drop area.

Project Shipboard Hazard and Defense (SHAD)

While much testing was conducted by the military, personnel were not exempt from being test subjects. Between 1963 and 1974, the U.S. Navy tested the integrity of their warships against biological attack by, you guessed it, attacking themselves. The miliary personnel aboard the ships were not notified and they were not provided with any protective clothing or equipment. They were attacked with nerve gases like Sarin, as well as toxic chemicals. The project was declassified in 2002. [Source]

New York City Subway

The testing on U.S. citizens of every race, creed, and social status was relentless. In 1966, a harmless bacteria was released into the New York subway system to find out how

vulnerable the system and its passengers were to biological
warfare. [Source]

Human Radiation Testing

Thousands of radiation experiments were performed in the United States. Most of the tests were carried out and funded by various agencies of the U.S. Government such as the Department of Defense and the Atomic Energy Committee (AEC). As with other testing, these experiments were conducted on the most vulnerable members of American society. Apparently using these people as test subjects without consent was a widely accepted idea among government officials and researchers. As you can see, the testing and experiments were widespread across the entire country.

Radioactive Iodine Tests

The "Green Run"

In 1949, this operation released radioactive isotopes including Iodine-131 and Xenon-133 into the atmosphere over Washington state. The test was conducted over populated areas and resulted in the contamination of three small towns. [Source][Source]

The Atomic Energy Commission

Throughout the 1950s, the U.S. Atomic Energy Commission conducted numerous radioactive Iodine tests in conjunction with various universities and hospitals. In 1953, in cohorts with the University of Iowa, the AEC did several tests that entailed newborns and pregnant women ingesting Iodine-131.

Pregnant women were given a dose of Iodine-131 so their aborted fetuses could be studied in order to determine at what point the placental barrier was breached. In another study, newborns under 36 hours old were administered doses of Iodine either orally or by injection. Their thyroid glands were then monitored for the amount of the substance that ended up there. [Source]

Another similar study occurred at the University of the Nebraska where healthy infants were fed Iodine-131 through a tube to measure the amount that ended up in their thyroid glands.

At Harper Hospital in Detroit, 65 premature infants were given doses of Iodine-131 in an effort to see if their bodies reacted differently from those of full-term babies. [Source]

Sonoma State Hospital

Between 1955 and 1960, Sonoma State Hospital was a drop-off point for mentally and physically disabled children. Parents could drop off their children for permanent care with no questions asked. CBS News' *60 Minutes* uncovered the horrors that occurred after such drop-offs. More than 1,400 children with cerebral palsy were given irradiated milk or spinal taps where spinal fluid was removed and replaced with irradiated gases. Every child with cerebral palsy that died at Sonoma State had their brain removed from their bodies without consent. Sonoma State Hospital still operates under the name of Sonoma Developmental Center. [Source]

These are just a few of the thousands of experiments that were conducted. I have no doubt that probably the majority of those tests were carried out in like manner. If these were things that were going on 60 to 70 years ago, do you ever wonder what's going on behind the scenes now?

Uranium Tests

University of Rochester

In 1946 and 1947, six people at the University of Rochester were injected with Uranium-234 and Uranium-235 to measure how much it would take until it damaged their kidneys. [Source]

Dr. William Sweet

At Massachusetts General Hospital between 1953 and 1957, eleven terminal patients suffering from brain tumors were injected with Uranium to determine if it was viable as chemotherapy for the tumors. Dr. Sweet went to his death in 2001 stating that consent was received for all of the patients by them or their next of kin. [Source]

Plutonium Tests and the Manhattan Project

Most plutonium experiments were conducted under the Manhattan Project. The Manhattan Project ran from 1939 to 1947. It was the government research project that developed the Atomic bombs that exploded over Hiroshima and Nagasaki during World War II.

Albert Stevens

Albert Stevens was misdiagnosed with stomach cancer. He showed up at the U.C. San Francisco Medical Center for treatment. Dr. Joseph Gilbert Hamilton was in charge of the Manhattan Project experiments in California. Hamilton had Stevens injected with Plutonium-238 and Plutonium-239 as a treatment for the cancer he did not have. Stevens underwent surgery that successfully removed a benign tumor from his stomach. Stevens never gave consent to the injection and was lied to about his tumor being benign. He and his family thought he had been treated successfully with the Plutonium and he lived for 20 more years having received the largest dose of Plutonium-238 by any person ever. His remains were acquired in 1975 without consent of his surviving relatives by Argonne National Laboratory Center for Human Radiobiology and dispersed to a national repository for people who died with radioisotopes in their bodies. [Source]

Simeon Shaw

Simeon Shaw was a 4-year-old Australian boy who was diagnosed with an aggressive form of bone cancer in January of 1946. His parents decided to bring him to the United States for diagnosis and treatment. He ended up in the care of Dr. Joseph Gilbert Hamilton at University of California Hospital in San Francisco. Working on the Manhattan Project, Hamilton and other researchers were trying to find out how and if the human body eliminated Plutonium. Simeon became ensnared in the study without the consent of his parents who thought he was receiving cutting edge treatment. He was injected with Plutonium-239 on April 26, 1946 and died 8 months later.

Elmer Allen

Elmer Allen was an African-American man and railroad employee who had fallen from a train and injured his knee. On July 18, 1947, he was injected with Plutonium in his left leg. He had been misdiagnosed with pre-existing bone cancer at 36 years old. Three days after the injection, his leg was amputated and taken away for radiological study. Elmer Allen lived until 1991 with numerous complications from the Plutonium injection including alcoholism, epilepsy, and paranoid schizophrenia. His surviving children and grandchildren still recount his life and sufferings. [Source]

Testing Involving Other Radioactive Materials

The experiments continued after World War II with other radioisotopes. The tests also continued to occur at universities, state hospitals, prisons and other facilities on the unfortunate lower classes of society. The tests were sponsored by the AEC, and some well-known corporations even got involved. There was no end in sight.

Vanderbilt University - Tennessee

820 pregnant women were given so-called "vitamin drinks". Unbeknownst to the mothers-to-be, the mixtures contained radioactive iron. The researchers sought to determine how long it took the isotope to breach the placental barrier. As a result of the testing, 3 children and 4 babies died of cancer. The women also experienced various symptoms from the radiation including, but not limited to, cancer and rashes. [Source][Source]

Walter E. Fernald
State School -
Massachusetts

Between 1946 and
1953, an experiment
funded by the U.S.
Atomic Energy Commission and Quaker Oats, fed 73
mentally-disabled children oatmeal that was laced with
radioisotopes. The test sought to conclude how the isotopes
were digested. The children were told they were joining a
"science club". The consent form sent to parents made no
mention of the radioactive ingredients.

In another experiment, malnourished babies were injected
with radioactive chemicals. Researchers then inserted needles
in their skulls and into their brains to collect cerebrospinal fluid
for testing.
[Source][Source]

Medical College of
Virginia

In the 1950s, researchers injected patients that had been severely burned with 50 times the acceptable amount of Phosphorus-32 for a healthy person. Most of the patients were poor, black, and were subjected to tests that included additional burning, experimental antibiotics, and injection with isotopes. There is no doubt this increased the death rate of the burn victims. The testing was funded by the U.S. Army and the AEC. [Source]

Utah State Prison and the University of Utah

From 1961 to 1962, blood samples were taken from 10 inmates, mixed with radioactive material, and reinjected into the prisoners. The researchers later produced papers stating that irradiated Phosphorus contributes to various forms of bone cancer.

The University of Utah conducted a total of 13 experiments involving more than 600 people between 1954 and 1972. More than half of the people involved were prisoners. [Source]

Irradiation Testing

Department of Defense and Dr. Eugene L. Saenger

For 11 years between 1960 and 1971, poor, black cancer patients received full body radiation and were told they were "treatments" that could possibly cure their cancer. Through the study, the Pentagon sought to determine the effects of radiation exposure in high amounts on the body. The patients did not consent to radiation and weren't told what was being done to them. One of the doctors performing the research, Dr. Robert Stone, expressed his concern about litigation regarding the testing. Because of his concern, he only used the patents' initials in his report so they could never connect themselves to the testing.

Dr. Saenger performed many studies throughout the 1950s and 1960s that were ground-breaking discoveries in Radiology regarding dosimetry and development of triage procedures for radiation victims. However, all of his research was tarnished by his crimes of non-consensual human testing on more than 90 poor, black cancer patients. Saenger defended that the tests were to see if the radiation could relieve the symptoms of the patients, but as many as 20 of the patients died as a result of the experiments. Others suffered from intensified symptoms including terrible pain and vomiting as a result. Isn't it odd that radiation therapy is still used as cancer treatment today? Dr. Saenger defended that the patients were terminally ill and the treatments were intended to try and improve their condition, but were never intended to cure them. Critics have said the tests were funded by the Department of Defense because the government wanted to know the effects of radiation on the human body. [Source][Source]

Dr. Carl Heller and the Buchenwald Touch

For those who may not know, Buchenwald was a Nazi concentration camp located in Weimar, Germany during the second World War. It was primarily a forced-labor camp and operated from 1937 until its liberation in 1945. The remains of the camp are a museum today.

For a decade between 1963 and 1973, Dr. Carl Heller performed tests on prisoners in Washington and Oregon. Heller was an award-winning, internationally-recognized endocrinologist. The AEC approached him and funded his work to determine the effect on radiation on the male reproductive organs. While Dr. Heller compensated the prisoners for their participation, he did not advise them of the dangers surrounding the testing. Some litigation did occur in the mid-70s and 9 plaintiffs settled out of court and split less than $2500.

Dr. Joseph Hamilton, who worked on the Plutonium experiments for the Manhattan Project at U.C. San Francisco said the experiments "had a little of the Buchenwald touch". Any such comparison is appalling for many reasons and indicates these doctors realized the horrors they were committing. [Source][Source]

Chemical Warfare Testing

In addition to radiation testing, the U.S. government also conducted hundreds of chemical tests on military personnel, citizens, and prisoners. In the name of science and medicine, countless people underwent tests, many of which resulted in suffering and death. For more than a century, from the mid-1800s through the the mid-1900s, the government covered up the testing for the most part. It wasn't until 1947 that real legislation happened to regulate human testing, and even then, it wasn't enough to stop it completely. [Source]

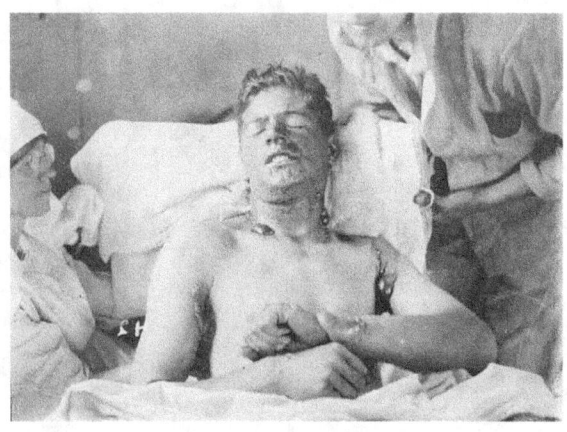

Mustard Gas

Between 1942 and 1944, the U.S. Chemical Warfare Service did several tests involving mustard gas. The purpose of the experiments was to test the effectiveness of military gas masks and other protective equipment, as well as the effect of the gas on men of different races.

Mustard gas had been used in the first World War by the Germans against the British in France and resulted in more than 400,000 casualties. The United States ignored the studies from World War I that concluded the gas also caused long-term health issues for survivors who were exposed to it. They continued testing.

Glenn Jenkins

In 1943, Glenn Jenkins was 17 years old. The U.S. Navy locked Jenkins in a gas chamber and filled it with mustard and arsenic gases. He could see the dome of the capitol from his location. He never fully recovered and was wrongly diagnosed with tuberculosis until a doctor experienced with mustard gas realized his symptoms were from lung damage from the gas. Mr. Jenkins remarked in 1993 about his neighbors who still did not believe his story. They did not believe the U.S. Government would do that to their own people.

Nathan Schnurman

Nathan was also 17. He agreed to help the Navy test summer uniforms. He arrived at an Army camp called Edgewood in Maryland where he was issued a gas mask. He, too, was locked in a chamber. A yellow mist poured in from the ceiling.

When his mask failed, he requested via intercom to come out, but was refused. Schnurman vomited into his mask and suffered a heart attack before he was dragged from the chamber into fresh air.

Russell O'Berry

Russell, another 17-year-old, was given a direct order to enter a gas chamber and threatened with 40 years in Fort Leavenworth if he refused after learning he would be testing the effects of mustard gas. He had just completed boot camp and was asked by an officer to participate in a secret experiment that would help shorten the war without knowing what the experiment entailed.

Just before entering the gas chamber with 9 others, Russell had passed a physical examination, the last one he would pass in the military or after that day. The mustard gas initially caused burning, blisters, and a hacking cough; however, Russell eventually went blind in one eye and ran a sandwich bar because he was unable to find better work. [Source]

Dermatological Testing

Dr. Albert M. Kligman and Holmesburg Prison

Between 1951 and 1974, Dr. Kligman conducted some astonishing dermatological tests on inmates at Holmesburg Prison in Pennsylvania. These tests were funded by; are you ready for some big names? They were funded by the Dow Chemical Company, Johnson & Johnson (yeah, the people who make Q-Tips and baby shampoo!), in conjunction with the U.S. Army.

Kligman patented Retin-A, a drug used to combat acne, but his career was shadowed by his architecture of the experimental research program at Holmesburg Prison. In 1966, Kligman in an interview by the Philadelphia Inquirer, stated in regard to visiting Holmesburg that "All I saw before me were acres of skin. I was like a farmer seeing fertile fields for the first time."

Kligman is said to have had numerous studies going constantly over the 23 years of the program. Inmates were paid a stipend to participate by more than 30 pharmaceutical companies. They tested medications, as well as chemicals including dioxin, which was an ingredient Dow used in Agent Orange. Prisoners, most of whom were black, were injected with the chemical to the point of suffering horrible skin lesions which went untreated for 7 months.

Prisoners later sued Kligman to no avail as the courts ruled that the statute of limitations had run out. It has been estimated that 9 out of 10 prisoners at Holmesburg during this time participated in the testing. The experiments overshadowed Kligman's career through his death in 2000. He maintained that no long-term damage was sustained by participants and expressed his disdain that legislation had halted the testing in the late 1970s. [Source][Source]

Continued Experimentation

Human experimentation continued with psychological experiments such as Project MKUltra which was a foray into testing different methods of mind control. The CIA claims to have shut down the project in 1973, but conspiracy theorists have attempted to show evidence that it is ongoing. Look out for the next book in this series which will focus on MKUltra.

This book is only the tip of the iceberg. I encourage you to conduct your own research. The rabbit hole is broad, but deep. I am supplying all of the links I can in the addendum at the end of this publication to get you started.

From the Author

Some of you may find the information in this book hard to believe. After all, we have not been conditioned all of our lives to believe our government would harm us. We've been led to believe quite the opposite. I submit to you that we *have* been "led" and "conditioned" though.

The things I've documented in this publication are backed up by declassified documents, court cases, and other documentation which proves them to be factual. Based on the sources presented, these atrocities happened. They were orchestrated and funded by the United States Government and relevant agencies. Let that sink in.

I ask you now to consider...where do I even begin?

First, let's consider the assassination of John F. Kennedy. I start here because this is where I first started my journey into the idea that the U.S. government lies. We have nowhere near as many proven facts about what happened on November 22, 1963 in Dallas, Texas, yet 78% of us believe it was a conspiracy. 78% believe the government lied in the "official" story.

One-third of Americans believe that the attacks of September 11, 2001 were an inside job. Yes, that they were orchestrated by our own government. Appalling, to say the least, but…

If all of this horrible testing is fact…what else is fact? What else have we been lied to about? What else has been hidden in classified documents or even destroyed? I think it's impossible to imagine.

So, let's consider some of the more far-fetched conspiracies…like chemtrails. Chemtrails are the idea that planes are spraying chemicals in the atmosphere to alter the weather and be tested as possible atmospheric weapons and shields. It doesn't see so far-fetched when you consider it after reading this book, does it? http://weathermodification.com/

What if we consider anti-vaxxers? This is a recent label slapped on people who refuse to vaccinate their children because they believe the vaccines are unsafe or may cause certain maladies. Do you have a renewed empathy for these people? It's okay if you don't…I'm just asking you to consider these things.

Do you think that a government that is capable of carrying out heinous experiments on its own citizens and cover them up is able to discredit those who disagree and make too much noise about its practices? Do you think the testing continues? I do.

I think there's a very important message that needs to be delivered to the American people. We need to understand that our government has deemed us expendable based on race, class, status, and other parameters. Our government sacrifices our native sons and daughters in wars it has funded and created itself. Our government, made up of men and women just like ourselves, took it upon themselves to deem certain ones of us unworthy of the inalienable rights given to us by God and risk our lives in experiments.

This government is the government from which the U.S. Constitution protects We The People.

If you enjoyed this book, please check out the next book in the series:

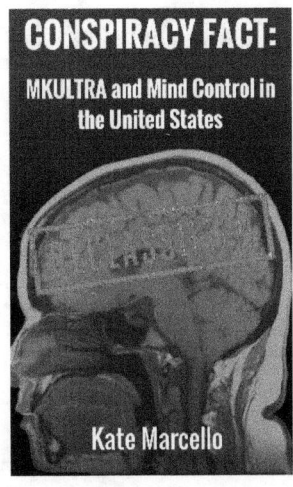

Mind Control in the United States? Hard to believe? The series Conspiracy Fact Declassified is back again to prove it happened.

Through declassified documents and various other sources, we further explore human experimentation. This time we zoom in specifically on mind control and the Top Secret government projects that examined this realm.

We name the names.

This compelling book is sourced throughout. You'll find out about how the U.S. ferried Nazi scientists into the country after World War II, and how that single operation became the catalyst for the creation of MULTIPLE experimental projects. You'll find out how those projects sourced more than 88 institutions nationwide to perform mind control experiments on unwitting citizens.

You will hear from survivors. Check it out on Amazon - http://amzn.to/1KzGGPL

Check out my blog: http://theydoconspire.blogspot.com/

Join the conversation on Facebook:

https://www.facebook.com/conspiracynontheories/

Addendum

1947 Memo revealing why radiation experiments were censored - http://www.dailycensored.com/censored-in-1995-1947-aec-human-radiation-experiments-memo/

Elmer Allen's Granddaughter - http://youtu.be/Sry_jcX6aiQ

Timeline of Laws related to human subjects - http://history.nih.gov/about/timelines_laws_human.html

Declassified Document Databases

http://www.archives.gov/research/declassification.html

http://www.foia.cia.gov/

http://www.theblackvault.com/

http://www2.gwu.edu/~nsarchiv/

http://vault.fbi.gov/

Links From Book Text in Order of Appearance

http://www.medscape.com/viewarticle/479892_1

http://www.ncbi.nlm.nih.gov/pubmed/19286295

http://pediatrics.aappublications.org/content/62/3/401.abstract

http://www.oddlyhistorical.com/2014/06/30/dr-leo-stanley-san-quentin-eugenics-experiments/

http://bit.ly/1GlZtMS -
https://books.google.com/books?id=kdFXAAAAMAAJ&pg=PA436&lpg=PA436&dq=6+leper+girls+syphilis&source=bl&ots=xVPXLWZZ9p&sig=ZZkYJE8XH53L6TInlC1ZddkyVGg&hl=en&sa=X&ei=ilHrVOf9NvL8sATJhYDICw&ved=0CD4Q6AEwBQ#v=onepage&q=6%20leper%20girls%20syphilis&f=false

http://www.ahrp.org/history/history.php

http://bit.ly/1Gm7S2T -
http://news.google.com/newspapers?nid=1955&dat=19100418&id=IC4rAAAAIBAJ&sjid=qJsFAAAAIBAJ&pg=6351,5079141

http://en.wikipedia.org/wiki/Unethical_human_experimentation_in_the_United_States

http://www.tuskegee.edu/about_us/centers_of_excellence/bioethics_center/about_the_usphs_syphilis_study.aspx

http://nypost.com/2014/02/01/behind-the-secret-plan-to-smuggle-nazi-scientists-to-america/

http://en.wikipedia.org/wiki/Jonas_Salk

http://www.ahrp.org/history/chronology.php

http://www.ncbi.nlm.nih.gov/pubmed/24769747

http://bit.ly/17s0CpV -
https://books.google.com/books?id=78dvvyqgi7MC&pg=PA36
&lpg=PA36&dq=Dr.+Alf+Alving&source=bl&ots=ADbppWt30Y
&sig=vFIzEPdkfC9fyT9wSk33yfN4ful&hl=en&sa=X&ei=XqzrV
LWSFdLbsAStvYGgBA&ved=0CFUQ6AEwCQ#v=onepage&q
=Dr.%20Alf%20Alving&f=false

http://en.wikipedia.org/wiki/John_Charles_Cutler

http://www.ahrp.org/history/chronology.php

http://icts.wustl.edu/icts-researchers/icts-cores/find-
services/by-core-name/center-for-clinical-research-
ethics/case-studies/dubois-case-study-4

http://fyb.umd.edu/2011/southam.html

http://jfk.hood.edu/Collection/Weisberg%20Subject%20Index
%20Files/C%20Disk/CIA%20CBW/Item%2001.pdf

http://blogs.telegraph.co.uk/news/timstanley/100104249/the-911-conspiracy-theories-arent-as-irrational-as-you-might-think/

http://bit.ly/17tK8gY -
http://www.jstor.org/discover/10.2307/1227417?sid=21105439358651&uid=4&uid=2

http://www.sfgate.com/news/article/When-U-S-attacked-itself-Government-tested-2864377.php

http://documents.theblackvault.com/documents/biological/bigitch.pdf

http://www.thesmokinggun.com/file/attack-killer-mosquitoes-0

http://www.publichealth.va.gov/PUBLICHEALTH/exposures/shad/index.asp

http://www.nytimes.com/1995/03/23/opinion/it-can-happen-here-and-did.html

http://www2.gwu.edu/~nsarchiv/radiation/dir/mstreet/commeet/meet8/brief8/tab_h/br8h6.txt

http://www.hanfordproject.com/greenrun.html

http://www2.gwu.edu/~nsarchiv/radiation/dir/mstreet/commeet/meet4/brief4.gfr/tab_p/br4p1a.txt

http://www.cbsnews.com/news/a-dark-chapter-in-medical-history-09-02-2005/

http://www.nytimes.com/1995/01/19/us/radiation-tests-used-some-healthy-people.html

http://www2.gwu.edu/~nsarchiv/radiation/dir/mstreet/commeet/pm04/pl4brf/pl4bre.txt

http://www.nytimes.com/1994/01/13/opinion/doctors-of-death.html

http://altbib.com/bak/dox/571.html

http://www.qcc.cuny.edu/SocialSciences/ppecorino/MEDICAL_ETHICS_TEXT/Chapter_7_Human_Experimentation/Case_Study_Radiation_Experiments.htm

http://large.stanford.edu/courses/2013/ph241/yeo2/

http://www.qcc.cuny.edu/SocialSciences/ppecorino/MEDICAL_ETHICS_TEXT/Chapter_7_Human_Experimentation/Case_Study_Radiation_Experiments.htm

http://www2.gwu.edu/~nsarchiv/radiation/dir/mstreet/commeet/meet11/trnsc11a.txt

https://www.prisonlegalnews.org/news/2008/mar/15/cheaper-than-chimpanzees-expanding-the-use-of-prisoners-in-medical-experiments/

http://articles.latimes.com/2007/oct/06/local/me-saenger6

http://www.nytimes.com/2007/10/11/us/11saenger.html?_r=0

https://bioethicsarchive.georgetown.edu/achre/final/chap9_2.html

http://bit.ly/1aj6LGJ - http://www.qcc.cuny.edu/SocialSciences/ppecorino/MEDICAL_ETHICS_TEXT/Chapter_7_Human_Experimentation/Case_Study_Radiation_Experiments.htm

http://history.nih.gov/about/timelines_laws_human.html

http://www.independent.co.uk/news/world/us-navy-tested-mustard-gas-on-its-own-sailors-in-1943-the-americans-used-humans-in-secret-experiments-patrick-cockburn-in-washington-reports-on-the-survivors-who-bear-the-scars-1497508.html

http://www.nytimes.com/2010/02/23/us/23kligman.html?pagewanted=all

http://www.washingtonpost.com/wp-dyn/content/article/2010/02/21/AR2010022104116.html

www.ingramcontent.com/pod-product-compliance
Lightning Source LLC
Chambersburg PA
CBHW062021280526
45787CB00005B/2190

* 9 781522 739982 *